T0353691

# Do you want to cure your
# **Irritable Bowel Syndrome?**
# Let me tell you how I did it!

Patricia Kenney, MSW, LCSW

**BALBOA**.PRESS
A DIVISION OF HAY HOUSE

Balboa Press books may be ordered through booksellers or by contacting:

Balboa Press
A Division of Hay House
1663 Liberty Drive
Bloomington, IN 47403
www.balboapress.com
844-682-1282

Print information available on the last page.

ISBN: 979-8-7652-5874-3 (sc)
ISBN: 979-8-7652-5875-0 (e)

Balboa Press rev. date: 01/16/2025

# Contents

# Contents

# Wake Up, Patti!

**"You can wake up, Patti. You're all done. You're fine.
You just have Irritable Bowel Syndrome."**

While I was happy to wake up from anesthesia after
my colonoscopy, and I liked hearing that I "was fine,"
I wondered what was so fine about Irritable Bowel
Syndrome. Irritable Bowel Syndrome, IBS, had caused me
considerable physical pain, panic, social embarrassment,
shame, and even trauma. The IBS was in addition to
two other digestive conditions: gastroesophageal reflux
disease-GERD-and diverticulosis. The doctors were not
very concerned about the GERD, commonly known as acid
reflux, that I was treating with prescription medication.
They also seemed unimpressed with the occasional,
painful bouts of diverticulitis, which is the inflammation
of small pouches that form in the lining of the intestine.

Of course I understood that the medical professionals who were caring for me during that 2019 colonoscopy were implying that I did not have a life-threatening or autoimmune disease, such as colon cancer, ulcerative colitis, or Crohn's Disease. But my gut discomfort and pain were not "fine."

This booklet discusses my experiences with IBS. Because as I, and everyone else who suffers from IBS know, there is nothing *"just"* and *"fine"* about having IBS!

**What to expect from this booklet**

While I do have both acid reflux and diverticulosis, it is the IBS that has been the most destructive in my life, and the most elusive to learn to manage. I have read a multitude of articles written by physicians about Irritable Bowel Syndrome. Most of these documents explain well the physiological causes and medical treatments of IBS. This article, from the NY Times, *What's the best way to treat IBS?* What's the Best Way to Treat I.B.S.? - The New York Times (nytimes.com) purports that the way to manage IBS is through diet and medications.

You will discover as you read this booklet that medical professionals are only partially right. As research scientists, they have no clue about the psychosocial component of the disease. In my experience, the omission of the psychosocial component does a tremendous disservice to their readers and their patients. But again, the psychotherapists are also only partially right. Apart from the medical and the psychotherapy professions, many other articles have been written about the use of neuropsychology and alternative medicine, offering yet another part of the solution to easing IBS.

I come to you not only as an IBS sufferer, but also as a seasoned professional mental health clinician, to offer you explanations and solutions that work. In my personal experience, they are successful only when used together, in harmony and synchrony with each other.

This booklet explores terms such as generalized anxiety disorder, panic attacks, neurobiology, the second brain, and the biopsychosocial perspective. To reach a solution to IBS, you will have to understand your own thoughts, emotions, and behaviors, how food and other supplements affect your bowels, and how your brain and bowels speak to each other. Every chapter in this booklet has a collection of Endnotes that offer more detailed explanations and interesting articles for further study, if the reader desires.

This booklet takes you on a journey through my own horrifying experiences. Perhaps you will be able to relate? I share how I altered my diet to discourage IBS. We will explore the world of psychology (how the mind works) and neurobiology (how the nervous system works). Finally, I describe how I applied concepts of meditation, affirmations, and visualizations to my knowledge of the human body and the mind to achieve control over my IBS symptoms.

That day in 2019 after the colonoscopy, the operating room nurse gently coaxed me to wake up from anesthesia. It was my own yearning to be free of IBS and to have quality of life that emphatically implored me to educate myself and *truly wake up*! Are you with me?

# My Story

I have IBS-D, Irritable Bowel Syndrome with Diarrhea. Some of the symptoms of IBS-D are:

- Frequent abdominal bloating, discomfort, or pain.
- Frequent and severe abdominal cramps that may improve with bowel movements.
- Frequent or changed bowel movements.
- Loose, watery stools.
- Mucus in stools.
- Feeling like your bowels are not empty after a bowel movement

**Interrupted journeys and quests for bathrooms**

I have had so many situations through the years in which I would leave the house feeling normal, only to develop a gut-gripping pain searing through my abdomen a few miles down the road. This pain is excruciating and forces me to search frantically for the next place of business with a public bathroom, hoping I will make it before soiling myself. This has happened while on dates with special people I wanted to impress, while heading to social gatherings, on vacations, at the grocery store around the corner, any time and everywhere. When I finally find and use the coveted bathroom, I feel much better. Believing that the ordeal is over, I put a smile on my face, and tell my companions, "I am fine now." But no sooner are we back on the road, the cramps start again, and I am forced to find another bathroom or risk soiling myself, as the pain is so great. And if I am really unlucky, this may repeat a couple more times before my bowels are completely purged and the pain finally stops.

## Social Embarrassment

One time I soiled myself with an IBS attack while heading to a party with people I didn't know very well. I ended up throwing out my underpants and spent the whole evening without underwear. Another time I was forced to go into the woods on the side of the road, while I was on a romantic date, because there were no bathrooms to be found. I will never forget the time I was in Iceland on a bus tour, and there was a two-hour drive through treeless, volcanic wilderness in Iceland when my bowels started grumbling. There was no toilet on that bus.

**Uncomfortable First Impression?**

My spouse and I were looking to join a new church and were invited to a dinner in the home of one of the church members. I was fine until dessert was served. Suddenly, an IBS cramp seized my gut. I went to the restroom and hoped for once that would be enough. But of course, it was just the beginning. The whole table full of people saw me get up and use the facilities multiple times. I was horrified.

*And the doctors say I'm "fine", that I "just have IBS"?*

There are literally hundreds of scenarios I have had to endure before finally learning how to manage this disease.

**Family History**

When I was a teenager, back in the 1970s, I saw my mother suffering from the same malady. I was disgusted and appalled by my mother. To avoid the pain and trauma of IBS-D she began to avoid socialization. I watched her slowly become a recluse. I thought that in some way she brought the illness on to herself, that she wasn't trying hard enough. I was arrogant back then. I was proud of myself that I didn't have that disease: I had a stellar digestive tract and I loved being around people. So 20 years later when my IBS began in my early-to-mid 30s, I vowed to not become my mother.

There were two ways I handled my IBS differently from the way my mother handled her IBS. First, I would not let the disease turn me into an antisocial recluse. Did I subject myself to much more physical pain, shame, and trauma because of this? Probably. Secondly, whereas my mother allowed herself very limited treatment options, I was open to multiple forms of treatment. My mother had tried Amitriptyline and Lomotil to control severe diarrhea and altered her diet when in the throes and aftermath of an IBS episode. She altered her diet only according to the way her mother, my maternal grandmother, also an IBS sufferer, taught her. My mother was closed to any new medical offerings, alternative medicine offerings, or any concepts of stress and anxiety management.

**Education matters**

Education is another way I am vastly different than my mother. I studied science and earned a BA in biology. I taught biology in high school. In 1997 I earned an MSW and became a clinical social worker psychotherapist. During my study and practice of clinical social work, I observed the inextricable connection between IBS and anxiety disorders.

As a previous biology educator, I easily absorbed concepts of neurobiology and how the gut–known as the second brain–is directly connected to the brain via nerves that deliver all kinds of messages. I discovered techniques to better manage and control these messages such as meditation, practicing gratitude, and positive mantras. I discovered that the use of probiotics and herbal alternative medicine can be useful to promote healthy bowel function and manage anxiety.

My mom thought diet was the cause and only solution to managing IBS. I studied nutrition and learned that my maternal grandmother, who was born in 1909 and died in 1978 was not the world's foremost expert on the best IBS diet. I discovered that our diet does play a crucial role in the management of IBS, but it is not the whole story. In Chapter 5 we explore how anxiety, specifically generalized anxiety disorder, is the *root cause* of IBS.

### Some personal information I really don't feel comfortable sharing

I was married for 17 years to the father of my children. I divorced him in 2000. I remained a single mother of three until 2010, when I remarried. My second marriage was to a woman. This turned my family life upside down. I had changed. My family didn't like my spouse. While my two oldest children handled it, my youngest, my second son, did not. There were estrangements. When I did get together with family, I would have a secret fear that fighting and arguing, and more estrangements might happen. Outside of my family, other people–church people–also created a fear inside me. The church people were brilliant, accomplished, educated, like-minded folks, but I guess I forgot that so was I, and I was terrified that they wouldn't like me.

# 3

# Important Terminology

I don't want to make this booklet too technical so we are going to keep fancy psychological terms to a minimum. If these terms and concepts fascinate you, please refer to the Endnotes for more information. There are a few terms that you should understand so that we can use the same language through this booklet.

**Biopsychosocial**

The first term I learned about 30 years ago when I started my master of social work program was the term is *biopsychosocial.* This term is the bedrock of social work, and is crucial to our understanding of IBS. Let's break it down:

- *Bio* refers to biology, meaning your physical body, your medical issues.

- *Psycho* refers to your psychology, which is your thoughts, behaviors, and emotions.
- *Social* has to do with everything outside of your body, everything that is not you. So that includes the material world (your house, your car, etc.) the natural world (plants, animals, insects, air, water, earth, etc.) and other people (relationships.)

Your mind (*psycho*) lives inside your body (*bio*) which interacts with the world (*social*.) But more importantly, your mind also interacts with your body, and vice versa. Your mind has a *conscious* aspect (things you are aware of) and a *subconscious* aspect (things you are not aware of.) The subconscious aspect talks to your body and your conscious mind, but it knows nothing about the outside world. A perfect example of this is how our digestive tract acts as our *Second Brain*, which is described in the Vagus nerve section on the next page.

**Biopsychosocial example**

The image below shows how *biopsychosocial* works. The dark blob is your conscious brain. The conscious brain talks to, and receives information from, the outside world and the subconscious brain. The lighter gray blob is your subconscious brain. The subconscious brain talks to, and receives messages from, your body and your conscious brain.

*Please note that your subconscious brain does not know what is going on in the world outside of you.*

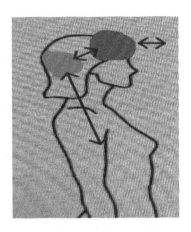

**Vagus nerve**

An important neurobiology term to know is the ***vagus nerve.*** Your brain and your body talk to each other via nerves. Your digestive system (your stomach, small and large intestines, liver, gallbladder and pancreas) and your brain communicate via a huge nerve called the vagus nerve. In fact, there are so many brain cells in your digestive tract, that it has been referred to as the *"second brain."* The vagus nerve goes straight from your subconscious brain to your gut. For more information, look at the articles referenced in the Chapter 3 Endnotes.

The *vagus nerve* carries signals from your brain to other parts of your body, to control breathing, the heart, and the digestive tract. The vagus nerve is the longest cranial nerve, and the messages are bidirectional. Bidirectional means that the nerve both sends messages and receives messages. The messages sent from the brain to the intestines and the heart are autonomic. Autonomic processes work automatically, and we do not have to make a conscious effort to make it function. As you will see in Chapter 6, it is my assertion that we can change these messages through meditation, visualization and positive affirmations. We can influence the messages that the brain sends to our bowels and aid in the control and management of IBS.

## Generalized Anxiety Disorder (GAD)

*GAD* is a persistent anxiety disorder that causes a chronic state of excessive worry, exaggerated anxiety, and feeling overwhelmed by everyday life. The GAD-7 questionnaire is a screening tool used by psychotherapists to measure the severity of the generalized anxiety disorder.

## Psychosomatic illness

A *psychosomatic* illness is a real illness, whereby mental or emotional symptoms trigger physical symptoms. *Psycho* means mind and *soma* refers to the body. IBS is a psychosomatic illness.

**Panic attack**

A panic attack is a sudden, transient intense fear response with a rush of mental and physical symptoms.

**Gluten Sensitivity, Gluten Intolerance, Celiac Disease**

Gluten is a substance found in wheat, barley, and rye. These three terms need clarification. To some, ***Gluten sensitivity*** *and* ***gluten intolerance*** seem to be interchangeable terms referring to the reactions or symptoms a person can experience after eating food that contains gluten. Other articles say that gluten sensitivity carries less symptoms than gluten intolerance, and that gluten intolerance and celiac disease are synonymous, because when you have celiac disease, your system is *completely* unable to tolerate gluten. This is the distinction I prefer.

With ***celiac disease***, if a person ingests gluten, their immune system attacks their small intestines and damages it. Celiac disease is a genetic immune system disorder that can cause symptoms that are much more severe than those from gluten sensitivity, and carries an increased risk of cancer.

# My Food Story

**I love to eat!**

I grew up in an Italian-American family where food and cooking were sacred. One of the greatest joys of my life is eating. You might have heard of a *gourmet*. A similar culinary word is *gourmand*. Both words are derived from the French language and both refer to someone who is knowledgeable about food and drink. Here's the difference: a ***gourmet*** is a person who is an expert in great food and drink that likes to share their knowledge about food and drink, while a ***gourmand*** is a person who is heartily interested in eating good food and drink. I enjoy cooking, eating great food, and watching TV cooking shows. Clearly, I am the gourmand!

Food is an important part of my existence. Finding and sharing recipes, cooking, and going to restaurants are a large part of my social life. For me, food is so much more than nourishment for the body. It is part of the fabric of culture, of tradition, of people's shared history, of how we show love to one another. Food is edible art! Food and all that it encompasses is a big part of my identity. Without it, I am not sure who I am outside of my profession and my relationships.

My favorite food is Italian and Mediterranean food like pizza, pasta, ravioli, lasagna, meatballs, marinated peppers and artichokes and olives, and any sandwich on an Italian roll. But I am also 100% American, so I love burgers, fried chicken, meatloaf, potato salad, green salad, fresh vegetables, and a roast beef dinner complete with mashed potatoes and brown gravy. I love the ultimate food holiday, Thanksgiving, dinner with so many delicious dishes. Summertime in New Jersey brings the best fresh-picked tomatoes, blueberries, corn, and peaches. Ecstasy is biting into a juicy, delicious Jersey peach that is so juicy that you have to eat it over the kitchen sink. Fresh-picked Jersey corn is so sweet and tender that you can eat it raw, right off the cob. Blue claw crabs and spaghetti in red or garlic sauce is a summer delight. All kinds of seafood, clams, scallops, shrimp, are available year-round. Heavenly!

But I would be kidding you if I ignored my sweet tooth: blueberry, peach, and lemon meringue pie, cupcakes, cookies, pudding, anything with chocolate. As an undergraduate majoring in biology, I would use a package of three Tastykake cupcakes as an incentive to prep for exams. A lot of memorization is needed in the study of a science like biology. I would split my notes into three sections. After memorizing each third of notes, I would reward myself with a cupcake. It was effective. I earned my BA *"cum laude:"* with honors (and cupcakes).

As much as I love sweets, I would happily trade any sweet for a snack food. The ideal snack food has four elements: it is salty, crunchy, greasy, and cheesy. For me, there is a fifth element that I can best describe as *"carby."* *Carby*, as I define it, is that feeling on the back of your tongue and throat when you swallow a starchy carbohydrate such as bread, pasta, and potato chips. Check out endnotes for more details about carbohydrates.

# 5

# Food is Medicine

**I finally discovered that food is also medicine.**

Every family is different. What I share is true for my family, and it may not be true for yours. My mother and grandmother knew that certain foods could make your tummy sick and other foods could make your tummy well again. And from my mid-30s to my mid-50s, the foods that made my mother sick, and the foods that made my mother better, were the same foods that made me sick, and then better.

In my family, eating a lot of fatty, greasy, oily foods triggers IBS. Eating too much food from the legume family–seeds, nuts, corn, and beans–does the same thing. The people in my family have an intolerance for lactose, so we don't eat too much cheese or milk products.

My mother taught me the foods that heal loose bowels or diarrhea are bananas, rice, and tea. She was following the recommendations of pediatrician Dr. Fe Del Mundo (born 1911 died 2011) who invented and popularized the BRAT diet (bananas, rice, applesauce, tea) that she created in the 1940s to help children with diarrhea. See endnotes for further information about the work of Dr. Del Mundo. At some point after 1950 pediatricians adapted the diet to include toast, and it became known as the *BRATT* diet. Read this article for more history of the inclusion of toast. BRAT Diet (Bland Diet): Benefits, Foods Included, and GI Uses (webmd.com).

As the 20th century moved into the 21st century, other articles argue that the BRATT diet isn't helpful, citing long-term nutritional defects. I contend that the BRATT diet is not meant for long term use. It is a temporary dietary tool, a starting point, to be used when your gastrointestinal tract is unwell. At the Memorial Sloan Kettering Cancer Center, they call the BRATT diet "phase 1." BRATT Diet Phase 1 | Memorial Sloan Kettering Cancer Center (mskcc.org) The BRATT diet has gotten me through many periods of ill health.

**A New Concept to Aid in Bowel Health**

In the early 2000s, Dr. Peter Gibson and Dr. Rita Shepherd created the FODMAP diet, an elimination diet which attempts to improve symptoms in functional gastrointestinal disorders. FODMAP is an acronym for Fermentable Oligosaccharides, Disaccharides, Monosaccharides, and Polyols. According to the articles, foods high in FODMAPs trigger the unpleasant symptoms of IBS, while the low FODMAP foods do not. Many of the high FODMAP foods-milk, cheese, legumes, wheat, for example-are triggering foods for me, while many of the low FODMAP foods-meat and eggs, for example-are on my "safe" list. But these FODMAP lists do not completely match up to my experiences. For example, the low FODMAP, (safe) list states that I can eat unripe bananas and peanuts. In reality, peanuts cause me abdominal distress, while eating *ripe* (not unripe) bananas continues to be a lifesaver for me.

**Foods that help me**

Slow it down!

- Oats: I have discovered that oats are also an excellent food to slow down and regulate bowel function. Oats can be a cold or hot cereal, or baked into bread and muffins using oat flour. Oats are magical in the way they slow down bowel function.
- Banana: To be effective, bananas have to be ripe to over-ripe. I eat banana and oats every day.
- Ginger and pears: Ginger and pears are great at slowing down my bowel function.

**Move it along!**

- Prunes: Prunes and prune juice, help my bowels move effectively.
- Fresh fruit: I eat at least one serving a day of another fresh fruit such as peaches, apples, and grapes to keep everything balanced.
- Other effective bowel movers: Yogurt, coffee, and alcohol.

Here's a scientific article about FODMAPs <u>Parrish Dec 12.pdf (virginia.edu)</u> and here is a simpler article to help you understand how an IBS sufferer can use the concept of FODMAPs to gain healthier bowel functioning. <u>FODMAP Diet 101: A Detailed Beginner's Guide (healthline.com)</u> I advise that each IBS sufferer experiment with these foods and discover what works best for you.

**Our food has changed**

About 10 years ago, I discovered by accident that I had developed a gluten sensitivity. This is how it happened: I went on a white flour fast in an attempt to lose weight. After three weeks, when I could stand it no more, I bought, cooked, and ate some imported Italian pasta. It was heavenly, but about two hours after eating it, I became ill. Every joint and muscle in my body was screaming in agony. My head was pounding; my stomach churning. It was a most unpleasant evening.

The next morning, I remembered that a test of food sensitivities and allergies is to withhold contact of the food in question for a few weeks, then re-introduce it back to your system. I couldn't believe it. Was I really sensitive to gluten, to all things made of wheat flour, to pizza, pasta, cookies, cupcakes, bread? To all the foods I hold dear, to the very essence of life itself?

Medical tests confirmed a gluten sensitivity but not celiac disease. My mother was offended and disbelieving. I couldn't eat her homemade pizza, pasta, cookies, or stuffing. "No one in our family ever had gluten sensitivity," she asserted. What mom had closed her mind to understanding is that the wheat of today is not the wheat of the 1970s or earlier. Today's wheat is a modern hybrid that grows to maturity quicker, to mass produce more product. If you would like to read more about this, see Endnotes for references.

**More changes in our food supply/
More bowel inflammation**

Not only are the crops we eat often altered genetically, but we also have to deal with pesticides, herbicides, chemical fertilizers, and the hormones given to the animals we eat. According to the National Institute of Health, "while the acute toxicity of certain pesticides is well documented, the subtler, long-term effects, such as inflammatory responses, have gained increasing attention due to their potential to contribute to chronic health conditions." (*Pesticide-induced Inflammation at a Glance,* National Institute of Health, <u>Pesticide-Induced Inflammation at a Glance - PMC (nih. gov)</u>) The hormones fed to beef cattle allow the animals grow fatter, faster. In turn, when humans consume these hormones in their beef and dairy foods, we become vulnerable to excessive weight gain, inflammation, and a host of serious life-threatening illnesses. We could write another whole book about the link between toxic food, and cancer, autoimmune diseases, birth defects, and autism. For more information, check out the Endnotes citations.

## Eat organic food

I have found it best to eat organic food as much and as often as possible. If a food product is labeled "organic," it means it was grown and produced without any type of added chemicals and without engineering of its genes. Do you scoff at the idea of choosing organically grown food? So did my mother. I once asked my mother if she knew what people called organic food when I was growing up, which was the 1950s-1970s. She shook her head. I told her "We called it *food.*" Back then, our food was grown without chemicals thrown on them.

**Probiotics**

Probiotics is another idea my mother thought ridiculous. Probiotics are bacteria. There are several strains of bacteria that live in our intestines. These bacteria are called "good" bacteria because they help us to be healthier in three ways:

- The probiotics munch our poop and help keep the digestive tract neat and tidy.
- Probiotic byproduct (yes, bacteria also poop) is not harmful to humans.
- Probiotics inhabit the available space in the intestines. If you do ingest bad bacteria, there will be no place for it to grow so the bad bacteria will not multiply and make you sick.

I have been using probiotics daily for about five years now. There have been several circumstances where people I was with have gotten sick with food poisoning or a virus, and I did not. I can't *prove* it was because of the probiotics, but it is logically possible.

**Healing Supplements**

There are many products available that can reduce inflammation and heal the lining of the digestive tract. I use some of the following products when recovering from any digestive illness. I use these products and I do not need pharmaceuticals when having tummy trouble.

- Aloe water ice cubes: I make ice cubes out of aloe water and consume them to ease nausea. I keep the ice cubes on hand in the freezer.
- Herbs and spices: When dealing with just the bowels, there are many herbs and spices that can help with inflammation just as well, albeit slower, than powerful prescription anti-inflammatories with all their side effects. For example, cinnamon, ginger, turmeric, cardamom, ginseng and rosemary can be used in cooking and baking. I like to drink Chai tea which contains cinnamon, ginger, cloves, nutmeg, cardamom and black pepper. I like rosemary on roasted meats.
- Tea: There is an organic tea I drink when healing from bowel inflammation called Mandela Masala. It contains rooibos, honeybush, ginger, cinnamon, cloves, cardamom, and black pepper. The tea is made by a company called SerendipiTea. This tea has helped me countless times to restore healthy bowel function.
- Deglycyrrhizinated licorice root extract: Deglycyrrhizinated licorice root extract, (DGL) helps heal the lining of the digestive tract.

# 6

# Patricia the licensed therapist, Patti the anxiety sufferer

There are two things that are true about all psychotherapists:

1. We had problems in our own life at one point. We sought education to help not just others, but ourselves as well.
2. In our training we learned what's called "the relentless pursuit of personal insight." That means we are trained to be able to delve deeply into ourselves, to understand not only our thoughts, emotions, and behaviors, but also what triggers those thoughts, emotions, and behaviors. As a psychotherapist, you can't help someone else unless you thoroughly understand yourself first.

Through this process of self-discovery, I was able to see that I suffered with generalized anxiety disorder (GAD). GAD is the disorder of worry. People with GAD worry constantly, about so many different things.

## Nature vs Nurture

GAD is also seen to run in families. Is it due to *Nature*, meaning it is an inherited trait? Or is it due to *Nurture*, meaning is it a learned behavior? My studies had led me to believe it is due to both. Erik Erikson, a German-born child psychoanalyst who emigrated to the USA, wrote books that held theories that were groundbreaking and have held the test of time. One of these is the belief that behavior develops due to the *interaction* of Nature (your genes) and Nurture (your environment.) Here's an article if you would like to read more about Nature vs. Nurture. Nature vs. Nurture in Psychology (simplypsychology.org)

## Personal Insight

Anxiety and worry are prominent maladies in my family history. Parents teach their children in so many direct and indirect ways how to handle life. My parents learned worry from their parents, and they taught it to me, not directly and not on purpose. Children learn more from their parents by watching what they do, than by listening to what they say.

I indirectly learned anxious behaviors from my mom as a child. Then as an adult my mom became a huge trigger for my anxiety and worry behaviors as you can see as you read this document.

This drawing is a good depiction of GAD:

I keep this drawing on the wall behind my computer in my office at home. The good news is that you can learn to manage GAD, and using my heightened and refined personal insight helps me to do that. This skill is not exclusive to therapists, you can develop it too!

**The bad news is that GAD is the trigger to my IBS.** The worry actually travels down to my gut via the second brain highway called the vagus nerve that I introduced in Chapter 3. Let's review that: The vagus nerve carries signals from your brain to other parts of your body, to control breathing, the heart, and the digestive tract. The vagus nerve is the longest cranial nerve, and the messages are bidirectional. That means it both sends messages and receives messages. The messages sent to the intestines and the heart are autonomic. Messages transmitted autonomically means we do not have to make a conscious effort to make the process function. But could it be possible to send messages consciously?

## GAD group therapy

In 2019 and early 2020, before Covid-19 hit, I ran a group therapy for clients with anxiety issues. I dubbed the group *Serenity Now!* The flyer advertised: *"Anxiety is mental, physical and emotional. Come and learn how to outsmart your anxiety."*

To measure generalized anxiety in my clients, I used an assessment called the GAD-7. The GAD-7 measures a score of 0-4 as minimal anxiety, 5-9 is mild, 10-14 is moderate, and anything over 15 is considered severe anxiety. Out of a group of 7 adults in pretest scores, 1 scored in the minimal range, 2 were in the mild range, 3 were moderate, and 1 was severe. Four out of the 7 individuals in the group reported having bowel issues.

That means that 57% of the individuals in the group suffered from both GAD and IBS.

I realize that my Serenity Now! observations are anecdotal, but as it turned out, journal research supported my observation that there is a link between GAD and IBS. Please check Endnotes for several articles to learn more. I go one step further and assert that most people with IBS also have GAD. What this means, is that if your physician diagnoses IBS, do yourself a favor and see a qualified, licensed mental health clinician, get a diagnosis, and begin treatment for anxiety. You will not be able to manage your IBS until you can manage your GAD.

In my anxiety group therapy and in my own life, I began to incorporate stress management, the practice of gratitude, the use of affirmations, and mindfulness into my everyday life. These techniques are very helpful in reducing overall anxiety. Once again, use of my heightened skill of personal insight and self-awareness enabled me to identify the source, or triggers to my GAD and the IBS attacks that followed.

**So... hurray for me...NOT!**

I had all this personal insight, knowledge of stress management, knowledge of biology and how my body and brain worked, and insight about my food sensitivities. But all this information was useless because I still could not control my IBS/nausea attacks. When I was younger, I could have social anxiety/worry/nervousness/insecurity all day every day, but it didn't show itself in my bowels, for all the world to see. I could keep it private and deal with it inside my head. I didn't know what had changed, and I could not fix it. If this is what is happening to you, please read on...

# 7

# The Final Straw

In 2019, after my gastroenterologist proclaimed I "was fine," I had several more incidents, both at home while dining with family, or away from home, in restaurants, where I would develop IBS-D, along with severe nausea.

There was one event that I will never forget. It was February 2020. My family came to my house to celebrate my son's birthday. Present were my spouse, my grown daughter and her husband, and my one son whose birthday we were celebrating. We had a tradition in our family to ask the guest of honor what he or she would like to eat for their birthday. My son chose African food that year. My spouse and I worked together, found recipes, shopped for ingredients, and prepared the feast. The feast was fun; we enjoyed it.

Halfway through the meal my stomach started to flutter and rebel. I felt nauseous. I stopped eating, of course, and tried to calm myself. When the nausea worsened, I excused myself, went upstairs to my bedroom and bathroom. I made some bowel movements and hoped that would ease the nausea. But it didn't. It became so severe that I was forced to stay upstairs, away from food and food smells, but also away from my son's celebration and my family. I missed the whole evening.

Eventually, after everyone left and hours elapsed, the nausea eased. I fell into a dark depression of hopelessness. Through the night and the next day, I did not leave my bedroom. I asked myself, what is wrong with me? Is this what my life is going to be like from now on? Why was this happening? There was nothing I wanted more than to enjoy my family, the people I loved most in the world, and enjoy some excellent food. I did not want to live like this. I contemplated suicide for the first time in my life. Eventually my spouse helped me move past the suicidal ideation the following day, but I needed answers and solutions.

The next day, I called my gastroenterologist. She did take my call, and she heard my story. My first question was, why is nausea now accompanying the IBS-D? The second question was, will I ever be able to socialize normally again? She had two responses:

- I needed therapy to improve stress management, and
- I needed further medical tests to determine the cause of the nausea issues.

The first suggestion frustrated me. Since I am a psychotherapist, I know the value of therapy and counseling; I live it in my everyday life. Furthermore, I believed I had already read at least as much as, if not more than, any therapist I knew on the topic of how generalized anxiety affects the digestive tract. Nor did I like the second suggestion: Please don't tell me I have yet another disease or chronic illness.

I researched whether there is a connection between nausea and IBS. And the answer was a resounding yes! There *is* a connection between IBS and nausea. See endnotes for two good articles. What a relief for me that I didn't have another illness. But why didn't my gastroenterologist know that nausea was a common ailment associated with IBS? At this point, I realized that modern medicine and typical psychotherapeutic techniques did not have the whole picture about IBS and therefore could not provide the solutions I needed.

But the doctor was right about one thing: stress and anxiety are connected to IBS symptoms. In fact, IBS is considered a psychosomatic illness. A psychosomatic illness is a real illness in which mental or emotional symptoms trigger physical symptoms. The connection between the anxiety of GAD and the painful ordeal of IBS became clearer.

# 8

# The Missing Link in IBS/ GAD treatment

**Quest for the missing link**

Finding the connection between what was going on in my head, and suffering those horrible, embarrassing, painful, humiliating, relationship-ruining episodes of IBS-D with nausea eluded me for years. Learning how to avoid my food sensitivities, and eating less food, even if it is nutritious, was a huge piece of the puzzle. Understanding the GAD triggers, that is, knowing what psychosocial events triggered my GAD, and using my stress reduction techniques, was key in reducing the frequency, intensity and duration of IBS-D attacks. But the attacks still occurred. One or two times a year was still too much. Something was missing in my understanding.

**What the doctors and therapists don't tell you**

After that humiliating family birthday dinner, I went into an episode of hopelessness and contemplated suicide. My spouse came to me and said, "This is not your fault." She gave me a video tape of a lecture by Dr. Joseph Dispenza entitled "Rewired: Understanding the Power of Your Mind." While Dr. Dispenza is a chiropractor, he is widely known as a lecturer, researcher, and author in the field of neuroscience. Dr. Dispenza asserted that a person could change and totally recreate new ways of dealing with difficult situations through the practice of meditation.

**Hebb's Rule**

Dr. Dispenza's theory centers around the concept of Hebb's rule. Hebb's rule was conceived in 1949 by Harvard-educated Dr. Donald Hebb, a psychologist interested in neuropsychology. Dr. Hebb's research bridged the gap between neuroscience and psychology. Dr. Hebb found that neural connections are strengthened when two or more neurons are activated at the same time.

Hebb's rule asserts that: *neurons that fire together, wire together.*

**Hebb's rule and panic attacks**

To understand how profound this discovery was for me, I must digress and talk about **panic attacks.** A person has a panic attack when their subconscious mind thinks they are in mortal, life-threatening danger. This subconscious belief triggers the fight or flight reaction and tells your adrenal glands to pump out adrenaline. Adrenaline can be very handy when you need a burst of energy to fight off an enemy or run away to save your life. If there is no enemy, the adrenaline just wreaks havoc on your body: you can't breathe, you get shaky, your legs go rubbery, your heart pounds, you may get nauseous. You might feel like you might be having a heart attack or that you might die.

I have taught behavioral techniques to dozens of clients to ease these panic attack symptoms. The technique begins with **self-talk.** Self-talk is a form of meditation whereby you talk to your subconscious brain. Remember, the subconscious brain does not know what is going on in the outside world. The subconscious brain knows what is happening in the body and can hear the conscious brain. It is the job of your conscious brain to speak to your subconscious brain (self-talk) to tell it that you are fine and there is no danger, so please stop making adrenaline!

Next fact about panic attacks: there is always a trigger and often the trigger is repetitive. A person who is phobic of spiders may have a panic attack whenever they see a spider. However, there is a secondary type of trigger, and this is where Hebb's rule applies. I knew this secondary trigger existed, but knew little about this trigger until I heard Dr. Dispenza's lecture. This secondary type of panic trigger has to do with time and place. For example: If a person has a panic attack after she gets in a car to drive to new place, then it is highly possible that in the future, whenever she gets in her car to drive to a new place, she will have a panic attack. I had a client once whose first panic attack was in the evening after the news was done on TV. For years after that, the evening news triggered panic attacks.

Coming back now to our study of IBS, I came to realize that due to Hebb's rule, my IBS attacks were repeating themselves whenever I was in a same or similar environment or scenario as the first IBS attacks...the first family dinner I had a severe attack, the first trip to eat dinner with church members...these events became wired-*connected*, that is-in my subconscious brain-to IBS-D with nausea. This understanding was profound, and it changed my life. My spouse was right. It really *wasn't* my fault! And likewise, back in the 1970s, it was not my mother's fault, either. This was also the beginning of resolving my resentments and confusions associated with my mother.

**But this realization *also* meant my work was just beginning.**

The subconscious brain-to-bowel connection was not the same pathway as the subconscious brain-to-adrenal gland pathway. The brain-to- bowel connection transmits along the vagus nerve. Dr. Dispenza taught that behaviors could change by using meditation. He recommended repetitive positive affirmations. If the subconscious grabs hold of the affirmations, he taught, the two events–IBS and being with people I care about–will disconnect and a new rewiring will occur.

## Rewiring my mind with affirmations

Dr. Dispenza taught that the affirmations needed to disconnect the wiring that triggered my IBS had to be specific and positive. The subconscious brain does not understand negatives, like "I won't have IBS anymore."

The type of affirmations I wrote to talk to my digestive tract are highly specific to my situation, and they are intended to be corrective. The affirmations are meant to create a *new* reality, a *new* way of being and functioning. And when the affirmations work, boy am I grateful!

**I created and recited these affirmations:**

*I can entertain my family I can plan, prepare, co-cook, eat, clean up and socialize with my family and relax into it with ease. I can stay healthy and vibrant, mellow and calm, and stay in the moment, every moment of this venture.*

*I can ride public transportation buses, trains, trams, Ubers, cabs, and airplanes while remaining healthy, full of vigor, and asymptomatic of any disease or illness.*

*I can spend time with family and friends, go on adventures with them, enjoy museums, theaters, shows, restaurants and walks with them, while remaining full of health and wellness.*

*I can enjoy all time off and remain healthy during my days off, holidays and vacations.*

I must start meditating at least 7 days before the time off to remind my body to remain healthy so we can all enjoy the gift of the time off.

I recited these affirmations 3-4 times a day. I said them with reverence. At the same time, I did not become desperate or neurotic (that means emotional) in my recitations. I envisioned my conscious brain talking to my subconscious brain. I visualized the affirmation traveling down the vagus nerve to my digestive tract. Over and over, every single day. Each time I had a success, I talked to my tummy and told it how proud I was of its performance.

This may sound silly to you, but it is all part of loving yourself and lovingly coaxing your body to function in a healthier way. I use these affirmations even now, not every day, but when I am preparing for a family or friend gathering, or a vacation.

## Successes, failures, strengths, and weaknesses

I want to be completely transparent about what has worked and what still needs work.

My **greatest success** was with my family, that is, my children and grandchildren. Since beginning these affirmations, I have not had one single family event ruined by IBS-D with nausea!

Also very successful are the meditations to prevent illness during my time off. The meditations for using public transportation, however, have had only **moderate success.** Any form of public transportation where there is a public toilet available has given me no problems, complete success. But riding a bus with no restroom onboard still triggers excessive bowel activity...not full-blown IBS but not complete freedom from discomfort in my bowels. The truth is, I have a tendency now to avoid any public transportation that does not offer a public toilet. But I acknowledge and fully understand that **avoidance of a phobic event is very effective, but it is not the same as mastery over it.**

Here is an interesting article about the pros and cons of using avoidance to manage phobic/anxiety symptoms. Rethinking Avoidance: Toward a Balanced Approach to Avoidance in Treating Anxiety Disorders - PMC (nih.gov). Maybe someday I will be able to overcome the IBS trigger of riding on a bus that has no toilet.

**Resolving Issues with Mother as IBS Trigger**

Resolving relationship issues are the most difficult of all. They can be resolved but it involves a process and that means it takes time. I was estranged from my parents, as per mom's choice, since 2018. I came to realize that my mother's staunch rigidity, her inability to think differently and try to solve her own IBS issues, stemmed from extreme insecurity, worry and fear. It was frustrating, to say the least. Furthermore, Mom's fierce dislike of my spouse was so confusing and hurtful to me; all attempts to fix it were unsuccessful. The estrangement did provide relief from mom as an IBS trigger. (The avoidance approach we just discussed.) Mom's death in 2021 ended any IBS triggers caused by her. Her death provided the ultimate extinguishment of "mom as an IBS trigger." Understanding mom's behaviors posthumously has brought a level of peace but remains an ongoing process.

**Successful Bowel Mastery Experiment**

I have had an interesting development in bowel mastery when preparing and going on a vacation. Recently, (April 2024) we were planning a trip to Quebec, and the plane departure was at a time where we would be traveling via Uber on the highway to the airport during the time of my usual morning bowel movement. These morning bowel movements are like clockwork and trying to go earlier is not an option. I was unable to move the departure time, so I needed another plan.

I decided that 2 weeks prior to the trip, I would start to get up 2 hours earlier, to get used to getting up earlier and hopefully making that morning bowel movement earlier. Four days before the trip, I had a meditative discussion with my bowels before falling asleep. I told my bowels that we had to be able to have our morning bowel movement between 5 and 5:30 AM on the morning of the trip. The next morning, I was awakened by cramping in my bowels at exactly 5:15 AM. I was blown away by this! My bowels did indeed hear me and effectively accomplished what I asked it to...albeit not the correct morning! I forgot to tell it which morning needed the change. Therefore, it thought I had to do this the following morning! I LMAO (pun intended) and told my bowels each night until the morning of the trip the exact morning we had to accomplish a 5 to 5:30 AM bowel movement. And my bowels succeeded on the morning of the trip! This experience was so empowering. Seeing that my conscious mind could control what was heretofore uncontrollable brought untold peace.

# Conclusion

What I have written is my personal story. I wanted to be able to share how I overcame IBS-D with nausea that was threatening to ruin my life. Other than the proton-pump inhibitor (Nexium) that I take for GERD, I use no other prescription medications to ease IBS-D.

I have found that the root cause of IBS-D is anxiety, specifically Generalized Anxiety Disorder, and that certain foods exacerbate the IBS D symptoms. Managing stress and anxiety is a huge part of the solution, and gaining an ability for personal insight is a must. Tweaking my diet, the way I eat and how much I eat, was also a big part of it. But none of these solutions worked until I realized that my vagus nerve was sending bad information to my bowels. And this information was sent behind my back, so to speak, on the subconscious level.

Understanding that the only way to correct this was to feed different messages, positive messages, to my body via use of positive affirmations, meditation, and visualization, is what changed my life and improved my physical, emotional, and mental health.

I hope this information can do the same for you.

Patricia Kenney, MSW, LCSW
patriciakenneycounseling.net

# Postscript

During the writing of this document, I decided to try another food fast. As you read in Chapter 5, ten years ago I unwittingly discovered that I had sensitivity to gluten when I fasted from eating anything made with wheat flour. This time I abstained for 14 days from most grains and white refined sugar. I allowed myself organic brown rice with my balanced dinners and oat cereal in the morning for fiber. Since I don't like the taste of brown rice, it was guaranteed I would not eat much of it. I was both scared and curious about what would happen.

After the first week, I had two glorious days when my short-term memory returned and became clearer than it had in the last 30 years, since grad school. Additionally, I felt a freedom from excessive emotions. I developed an overwhelming sense of well-being. I found I could drink a glass of wine at dinner without pain or burning in my digestive tract.

My immediate thoughts were of inflammation, or rather, the lack of inflammation. The fact that I could have a glass of wine again, and I could think and process thoughts, emotions, and memories superbly, pointed to the possibility that all grain products must cause a level of inflammation, throughout my entire body.

I did some research to discover that most ancient civilizations would not have survived without the consumption of grains. But as a spiritual practice, some cultures frowned upon the use of grains: As it was written in the book *The Way of Qigong*, ancient Daoist mythology believes the principle of "avoiding the 5 grains." These grains were rice, millet, wheat, oats, and beans. (Today we do not think of beans as a grain.) These grains were thought to cut off life, rot your organs, and destroy your chances for eternal life. Fourth century Daoists warn that "the stench of these grains vexes the soul and stops the embryonic breath." Indigenous people warn to avoid food with gluten or wheat, <u>Ancestral Food-Ways — WELLFORCULTURE</u>, and Jews were forbidden to eat grains during Passover.

Admittedly, while I am not ready to give up all grains all the time, this little experiment has provided much food for thought.

# Endnotes

## 1 Wake up, Patti!

1   The term *Irritable Bowel Syndrome*, IBS, was first used by the medical profession in 1944 to describe abdominal pain, bloating, gas accompanied by diarrhea, (IBS-D) constipation (IBS-C) or both (IBS-mixed). Before 1944, similar symptoms were referred to as IBS colitis, mucous colitis, spastic colon, nervous colon, and spastic bowel. John Hopkins Medicine (www.johnshopkinsmedicine.org), National Institutes of Health (www. Niddk.nih.gov)*Historical viewpoint on the irritable bowel syndrome* Abstract pubmed.ncbi.nlm.nih.gov

2   *Ulcerative Colitis*, UC is a serious, chronic condition in which inflammation and ulcers occur on the lining of the large intestine and rectum. With UC, the cause of the inflammation stems from problems in the immune system. While UC itself is not life-threatening, people with UC are more likely to get colon cancer, and there are many complications arising from UC that can be life threatening: such as anemia, dehydration, and perforated bowel. www. mayoclinic.org. www.nuddk.nih.gov, www.webmd.com.

3   While IBS occurs in the colon, and UC can occur in the colon and rectum, *Crohn's Disease* can occur throughout the whole digestive tract, causing inflammation and irritation from the mouth through to the anus. Like UC, Crohn's is thought to be caused by problems in the immune system. Crohn's Disease is usually not fatal, but can it can cause fatal complications, and can shorten life expectancy. www. niddk.nih.gov, https://pubmed.ncbi.nlm.nih.gov, www. mayoclinic.org.

4   A brief word about gastroesophageal reflux disease, commonly called GERD or simply acid reflux. The medication I use, esomeprazole is effective, but I persistently wish I could get off of it. There are many articles written about the long-term use of proton pump inhibitors. Researchers have claimed that proton pump inhibitors can cause bone fracture, kidney disease, gastrointestinal infections, magnesium deficiency, and gastric cancer, and it can impair absorption of iron, calcium, and B12. Proton pump inhibitors: Understanding the associated risks and benefits of long-term use | American Journal of Health-System Pharmacy | Oxford Academic (oup.com), www.ncb.nlm.nih.gov, Advantages and Disadvantages of Long-term Proton Pump Inhibitor Use (jnmjournal.org) I have experienced low iron, calcium, and B12. For this reason, I take daily supplements of iron, calcium, magnesium, and B12, and I have my blood levels checked annually. On several occasions I have tried to replace the proton pump inhibitor with use of supplements, but with no success. If I succeed some day at getting off esomeprazole, you will be the first to know!

5   Small bulging pouches in the intestinal lining are called diverticula. They are a common occurrence of people over 40 yrs. These bulging pouches are thought to be created by eating a diet low in fiber. So basically, white, refined wheat flour is the culprit. Eat more whole grains when you crave food made from white flour. www.mayoclinic.org, www.nhsonform.scot.

## 2  My Story

1   Amitriptyline is a type of antidepressant that improves mood by increasing serotonin levels in the brain. It is also known to help with nerve pain and regulate bowel activity in people with IBS. While physicians still prescribe amitriptyline for IBS, the FDA has not approved it for this

use. When a physician prescribes a medication not approved for a certain illness, this is called prescribing "off label." It is a common practice. www.ahrq.gov, medicalnewstoday.com, www.isrctn.com.

2 Lomotil is a prescription drug used to treat diarrhea. It is considered a controlled substance because it contains a narcotic called diphenoxylate, which at low dose controls diarrhea. www.Goodrx.com.

## 3 Important Terminology

www.webmd.com, myclevelandclinic.org, "What to know about the gut brain link" https://www.webmd.com/digestive-disorders/what-to-know-about-gut-brain-link.

"Think Twice: How the Gut's "Second Brain" Influences Mood and Well-Being" https://www.scientificamerican.com/article/gut-second-brain/.

## 4 My Food Story

For more information about the history of gourmet vs gourmand, you can read this article in *The Atlantic*. https://www.theatlantic.com/magazine/archive/1956/04/gourmet-or-gourmand/641733.

## 5 Food Is Medicine

1 "Let food be thy medicine and medicine be thy food." I borrowed this concept that originally came from the great Greek physician Hippocrates, who lived from 460 BC to 377 BC. Celebrating Ancient Greek Thoughts on Food and Health - Food Studies Institute

2  Del Mundo, Fe - The Ramon Magsaysay Award Foundation - Honoring greatness of spirit and transformative leadership in Asia (rmaward.asia)

3  Biography of Fe del Mundo, Noted Filipino Pediatrician (thoughtco.com)

4  https://theceliacmd.com/celiac-disease-and-gluten-sensitivity-update-for-providers.

5  The Grainstorm Heritage Baking Company out of Canada explains the change in our wheat crops very well. Please check out their website: https://grainstorm.com/pages/modern-wheat. And while you are at it, you may be able to enjoy some of their ancient grain flour products.

6  Hormonal residues in chicken and cattle meat: A risk threat the present and future consumer health - ScienceDirect

7  www.SerenndipiTea.com 73 Plandome Rd. Manhasset, NY 11030 1-888-832-5433. I order my Mandela Masala tea from the website.

8  Carbohydrates, or carbs, are sugar molecules. Along with proteins and fats, carbohydrates are one of three main nutrients found in foods and drinks. Your body breaks down carbohydrates into glucose. Glucose, or blood sugar, is the main source of energy for your body's cells, tissues, and organs. Glucose can be used immediately or stored in the liver and muscles for later use. Carbohydrates: MedlinePlus

# 6 Patricia the licensed therapist, Patti the anxiety sufferer

1  Stress, Anxiety, and IBS: Stress Relief, Anxiety Treatment, and More (webmd.com)

2  Anxiety and IBS revisited: ten years later - PMC (nih.gov)

3  IBS and Anxiety - The Gut-Brain Connection, Symptoms, and Treatments (mindsethealth.com)

# 7 The Final Straw

1   Does IBS cause nausea? Symptoms, causes and treatment (medicalnewstoday.com)
2   Experiencing IBS and Nausea? Discover Causes and Treatment (healthline.com)

# 8 The Missing Link in IBS/GAD treatment

1   Dr. Joe Dispenza's website is www.drjoedispenza.com. His videos are available on his website for a fee.
2   Dispenza, Joe Dr.(2012) *Breaking the Habit of Being Yourself How to Lose Your Mind and Create a New One* Carlsbad, California: Hay House, Inc.
3   Writing positive affirmations and practicing gratitude go hand in hand. Positive affirmations are often taught along with a concept called "*practicing gratitude*." Practicing gratitude is showing appreciation and thankfulness to a person, to god, or to a situation. What is Gratitude and Why Is It So Important? (positivepsychology.com)

# Postscript

1   Cohen, Kenneth S. (1997) *The Way of Qigong* New York: Ballantine Books, pp 4, 299-300.
2   Bigu – Daoist Fasting | Daoist Gate

Printed in the United States
by Baker & Taylor Publisher Services